This Walker book belongs to:

_____

_____

_____

For Joss, who knows
all about it, too
J.M.

For Pea
K.M^cE.

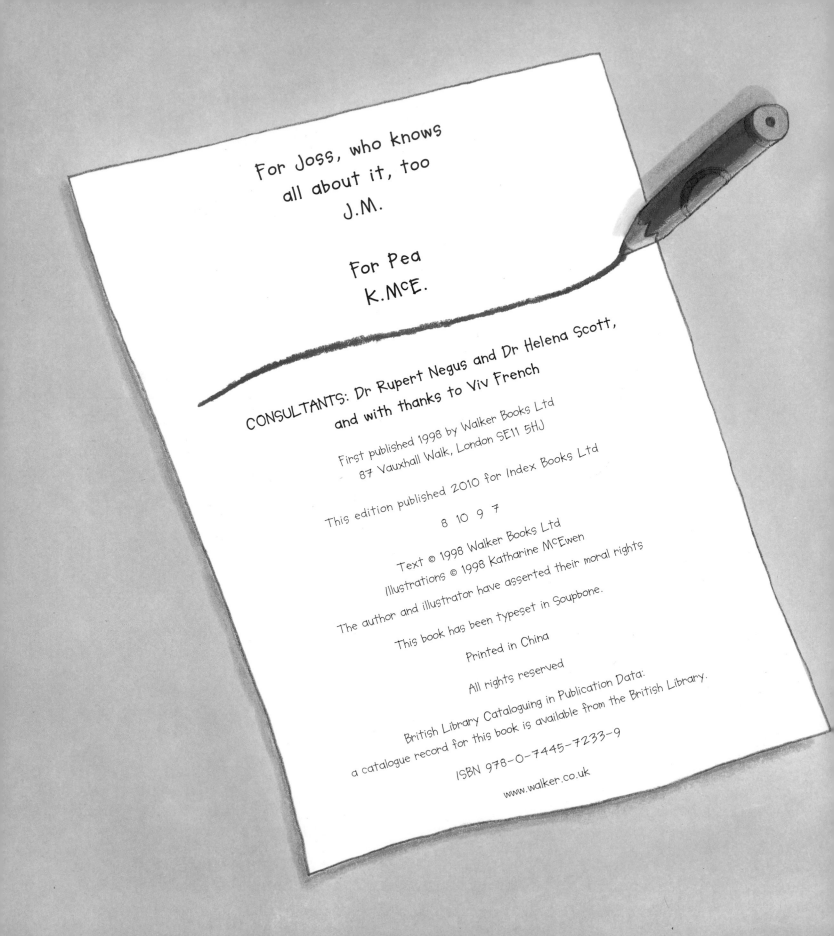

CONSULTANTS: Dr Rupert Negus and Dr Helena Scott,
and with thanks to Viv French

First published 1998 by Walker Books Ltd
87 Vauxhall Walk, London SE11 5HJ

This edition published 2010 for Index Books Ltd

8 10 9 7

Text © 1998 Walker Books Ltd
Illustrations © 1998 Katharine McEwen
The author and illustrator have asserted their moral rights

This book has been typeset in Soupbone.

Printed in China

British Library Cataloguing in Publication Data:
a catalogue record for this book is available from the British Library.

ISBN 978-0-7445-7233-9

www.walker.co.uk

I KNOW WHERE MY FOOD GOES

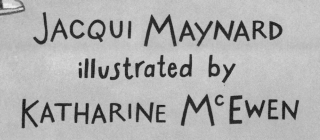

JACQUI MAYNARD

illustrated by

KATHARINE McEWEN

WALKER BOOKS

AND SUBSIDIARIES

LONDON · BOSTON · SYDNEY · AUCKLAND

Sam charged into the kitchen. "What's for lunch, Mum? I'm starving!"

"Hmmm... let's see," said Mum. "Stewed slugs? A nice plate of grilled worms in mud sauce?"

6

"I know," she said.
"How about pizza,
with strawberry
ice-cream for
afters?"

Sam grinned.
"YUM! My mouth's
gone all watery!"

"That's because it's getting
ready to eat something,"
said Mum. "Lay the table
for me, will you Sam?"

Sam got out some knives and forks. "Yeah," he said, "I know all about that. The watery stuff's called sal...sal... something."

"**Saliva**," said Mum. "Your body makes around 1.5 litres of it every day — that's about the same as eight glasses of milk!"

"Oh, right," said Sam. "But I know what **saliva** does. It makes food go all squishy so I can swallow it!"

"Yes, it does," said Mum. "But what else should you do before you swallow food?"

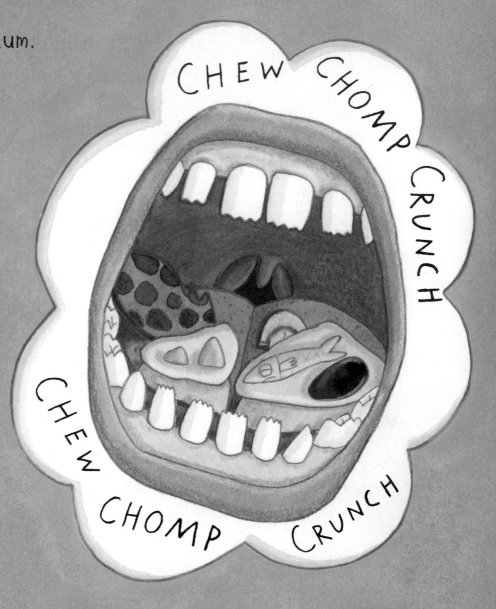

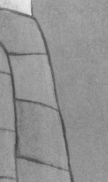

"**CHEW** it and **CHOMP** it and **CRUNCH** it all up," shouted Sam.

"And when it's all soft and slimy I swallow it, and it goes all the way down the food tube from my mouth to my **stomach!**"

"Right again," said Mum, handing Sam some plates.
"There's another word for your food tube,
though, isn't there?"

"Yes," said Sam. "It's an os...os...ostrich."

"Well, nearly," said Mum.
"It's called an
oesophagus."

Sam laughed. "I bet an ostrich has got a long **oesophagus**!"

"I expect it has," said Mum, "and a really skinny one, too. Yours is about half as long as your arm, and only as wide as your thumb!"

"And guess what," she said, as she put
the pizza in the oven, "even if you're standing
on your head, your food still goes straight
to your **stomach**. Don't try eating upside down
though, will you, or you might choke!"

"Course I won't," said Sam.
"But does it really?"

"Yes, really," said Mum.
"The food doesn't just
slide down your **oesophagus**,
the muscles inside it squeeze
the food along, just like
you squeeze toothpaste
out of a tube."

"Oh," said Sam.
"OK."

"But I know what happens next," Sam said,
putting two glasses on the table.
"My **stomach** is like a big stretchy bag.
And it squishes and squashes
the food round and round
until it's all gloopy
and gloppy, like soup."

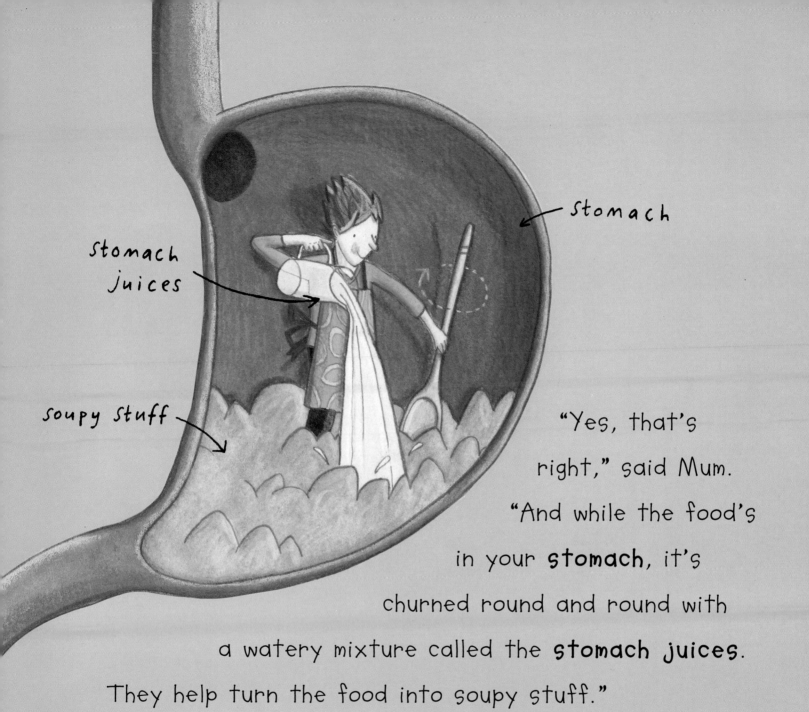

stomach

stomach juices

soupy stuff

"Yes, that's right," said Mum. "And while the food's in your **stomach**, it's churned round and round with a watery mixture called the **stomach juices**. They help turn the food into soupy stuff."

"Yeah," said Sam, "that's what I'm saying. And..."

"AND if you swallow lots of air
or fizzy drinks with your food,"
said Mum, filling up the water
jug, "you get air in your
stomach. And sometimes
the air comes rushing
back up again,
and you..."

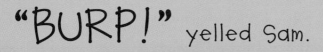

"BURP!" yelled Sam.

"We have burping contests at school."

"Oh, do you?" said Mum.

"Well that's why we're not having fizzy drinks!" And she put the water jug down on the table.

"Anyway, I wasn't going to tell you about the burping," said Sam, huffily.
"I was going to tell you what happens next. What happens next is the soupy stuff squirts out of my **stomach** into another tube."

"That's right," said Mum.
"There's a special muscle at the bottom of your stomach that works like a tap. It lets the soupy stuff out a bit at a time."

"Yes," said Sam quickly.
"And the tube it goes into
is called the **intestine**."

"Right again," said Mum, "though there are
really two bits to the **intestine**. This first bit
is called the **small intestine**, but it's not all
that small — in fact, it's about 5 metres long!"

"WOW!" said Sam.

"That's about as long as...as..."

"Hmmm," said Mum, thinking about it.
"I don't know what it's as long as either,
but it's about as tall as a giraffe.
And it's all folded up like spaghetti
in a bowl, so it fits inside you."

"The **small intestine** is where all the good things in the soupy stuff get taken into your body," explained Mum.

"That's what **digestion** is," she added, putting a big bowl of salad on the table.
"It's the way your body breaks down food and takes the goodness out of it, to give you energy and help you grow."

Sam sighed. "And that's why you're always saying green stuff like spinach is good for me," he said. "YUCK! I hate spinach! It's all slippery and slimy and it tastes like..."

Yuck!

"Yes, yes, all right," said Mum. "But vegetables really are good for you — they've got **vitamins** in them, and you need **vitamins** to keep you strong and healthy."

"I know, I know!" Sam sat down at the table.
"But I know something else that happens
in my **intestine**," and he giggled.
"There's gassy stuff in it, too,
isn't there? 'Cos that's
why I fart."

"Well, yes, there is," said Mum.
"The gas comes from the bits of food
that aren't used up in your **small intestine**."

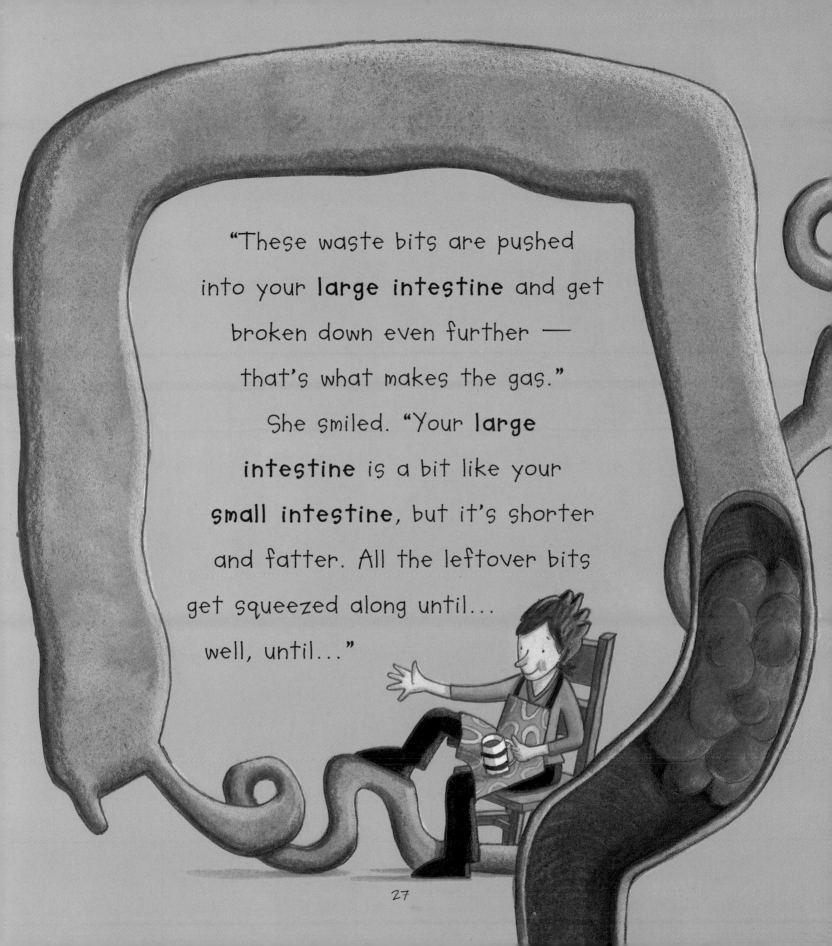

"These waste bits are pushed into your **large intestine** and get broken down even further — that's what makes the gas." She smiled. "Your **large intestine** is a bit like your **small intestine**, but it's shorter and fatter. All the leftover bits get squeezed along until... well, until..."

27

"Until they reach my bottom," said Sam,
feeling very pleased with himself.
"And that's when I have to poo!"
"See," he said, "I told you I knew
all about it, didn't I!"

saliva in mouth

Stomach and
Stomach juices

oesophagus

large intestine

small intestine

Sam

Index

Look up the pages to find out about all these food things.